The

NYSTROM

Nystronaut

ATLAS

M000009224

NYSTROM

DIVISION OF HERFF JONES, INC.

Executive Editors	Charles Novosad
	Tina Tinkham Garrison
Project Manager	Joan Pederson
Cartographic Manager	Christine D. Bosacki
Character Illustrations	Jeff Stock
Neighborhood Illustrations	Skip Baker
Nystrom Computer Cartography	Bonnie Jones
	Charlaine Wilkerson
	Phyllis Kawano
Photographic Research	Charlotte Goldman
	Susana Darwin
Book Design	The Quarasan Group, Inc.
Educational Consultant	Dr. JoAnne Buggey

For information about ordering this atlas and other components of the Exploring Where & Why program, call toll-free 800-621-8086.

1999 Edition
Copyright © 1998 NYSTROM Division of Herff Jones, Inc.
3333 Elston Avenue, Chicago, Illinois 60618

10 9 8 7 6 5 4 3 2   01 00 99 98

ISBN: 0-7825-0662-3   Product Code Number: 9A97B
Printed in U.S.A.

Contents

This list is called the table of contents.

Where do you live?

Wow! There's your world in the distance.

The earth seen from above the moon

Closer in, we can pick out your country.

Outline added around the United States

State boundary lines added

Closer yet! Now we can pick out states.

If we zoom in, we can see how Earthlings live.

This community and yours are not exactly the same. But they are alike in many ways.

Which community is like

Boston, Massachusetts

How tall are the buildings in YOUR community?

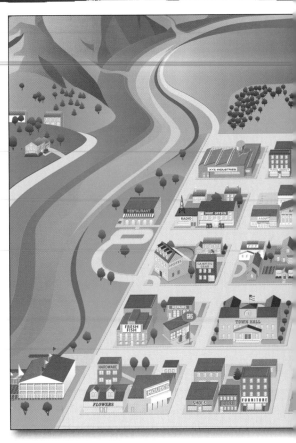

Communities come in many sizes. Some are big cities. Others are very small.

Town in western Wyoming

Is the land flat where you live? Or is it hilly?

Suburb near Phoenix, Arizona

Which of these communities looks most like yours?

How are they alike?

Rural community east of Sacramento, California

Office building

How many places like these can you find in the drawing?

This community has places to live, work, learn, and shop. So do most other communities.

Flower shop

School

House

Grocery store

Do you live near places like these? Which ones?

Factory

What do people make

Jars of baby food

What does that stuff taste like?

Many communities have factories. But factories are not the only places where things are made.

Hand-carved furniture

Computer parts

Baskets woven from grass

New houses

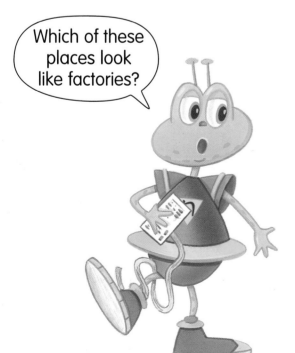

Which of these places look like factories?

What do you mean by "factory"?

Maps drawn with computers

What do people buy here?

Green food looks fun to eat! Is it good for you?

Fresh food

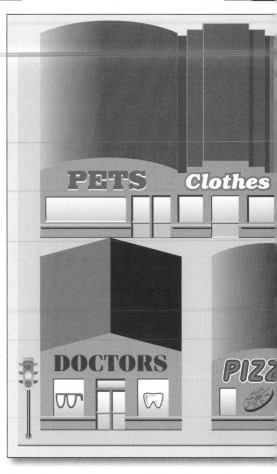

People meet some of their needs and wants in stores and offices. They may buy things near home, or downtown, or at shopping malls.

Medicine

Movie tickets

Do Earthlings pay for dental care and other services?

Dental checkup

Clothing

Can you find places like these in the drawing?

Dolls and other toys

Firefighters putting out a fire

People who have jobs in the town hall work for the community. So do other people.

Garbage collector removing trash

Who else helps the community?

Librarian listening to a question

community?

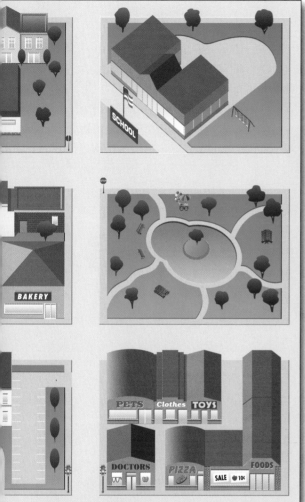

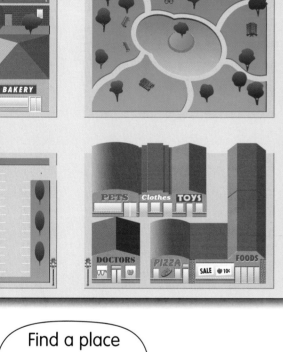

Police officer writing
a traffic ticket

Judge conducting a trial

Find a place
in the drawing
where a crossing
guard works.

Crossing guard stopping traffic

How do globes and

The earth looks like this from space.

A globe is a model of the earth.

Which is easier to read: a map or a peeled globe?

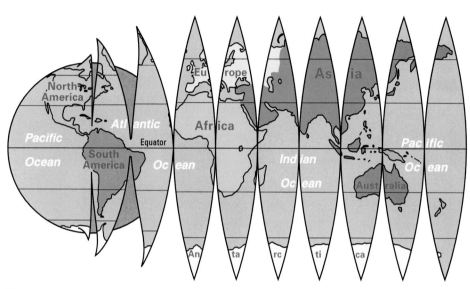

Only a peeled globe could show the whole world at once.

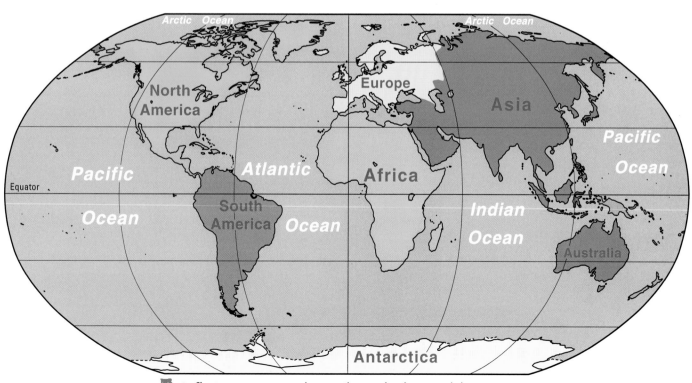

A flat map can show the whole world at once.

What is a map?

1 **View from the ground** Here's how you see buildings most of the time.

Find this library in views 2, 3, and 4.

2 **Bird's–eye view** Birds in flight look down at an angle.

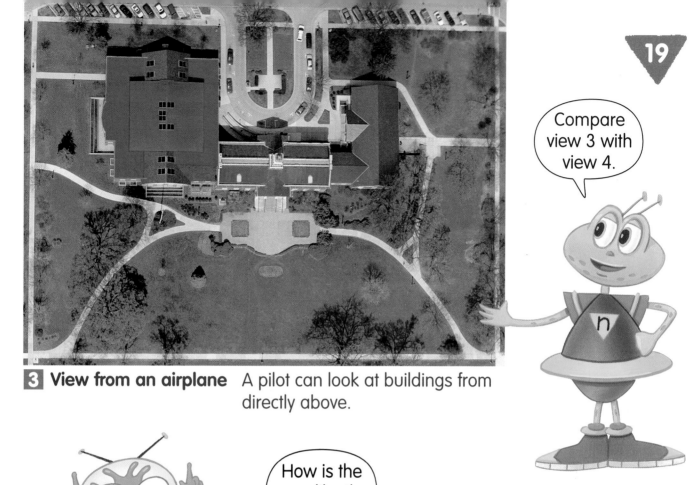

Compare view 3 with view 4.

3 **View from an airplane** A pilot can look at buildings from directly above.

How is the map like the photo?

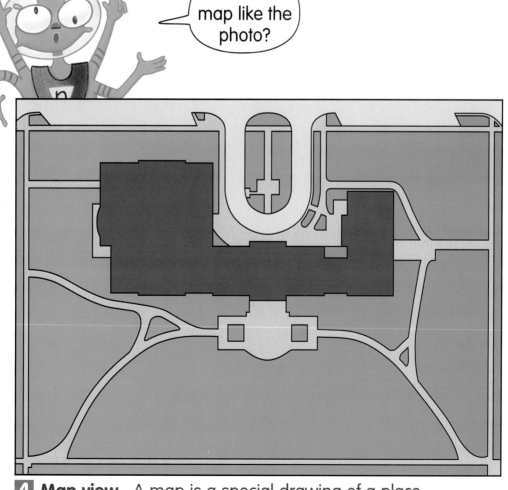

4 **Map view** A map is a special drawing of a place seen from directly above.

Coastlines Black lines between land and water show coastlines.

Rivers Wavy lines on land show rivers.

Lakes How can you tell lakes from oceans?

places?

Find the meanings of these six terms in the glossary.

Sawtooth Mountains

Mountains Gray shadows show mountains and hills.

Pittsburgh

Cities Dots show where cities are located.

On the ground, you see a sign, not a line!

Wyoming

Nebraska

Boundaries What color are boundary lines?

Where in the world is

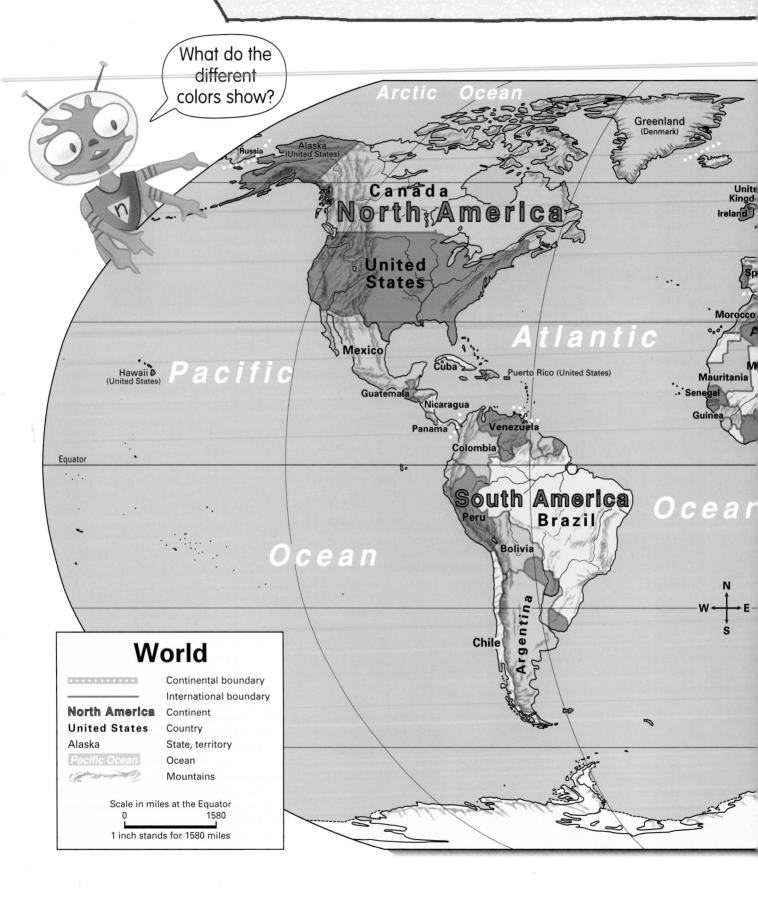

What do the different colors show?

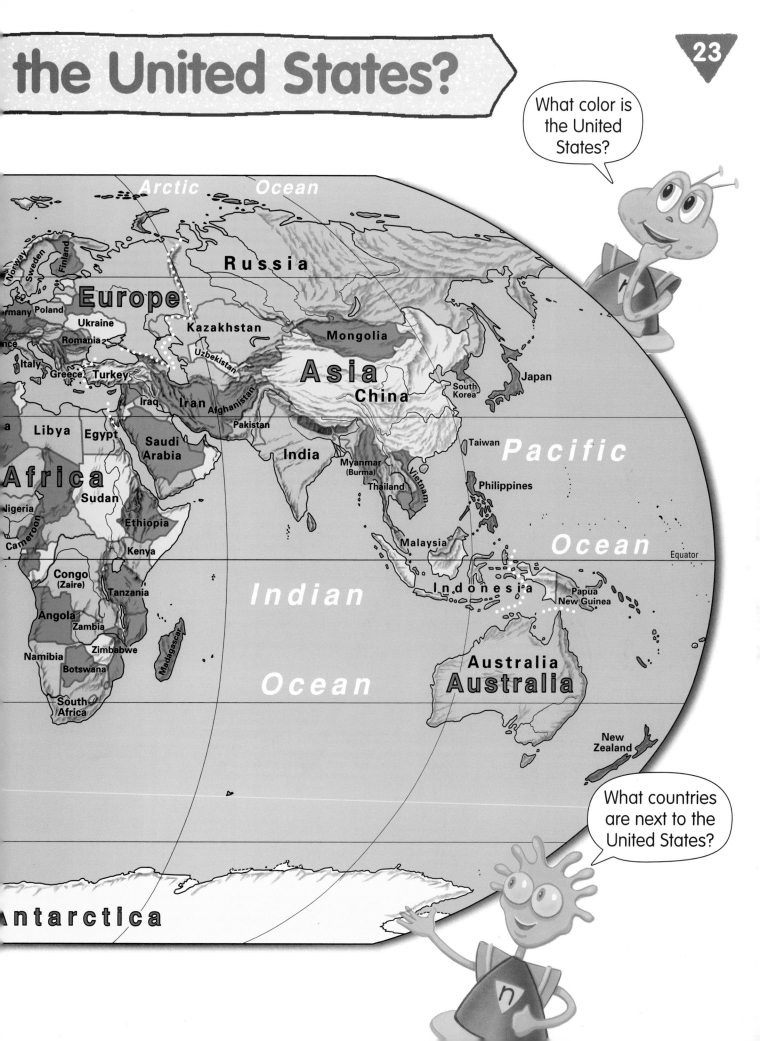

Where is your state?

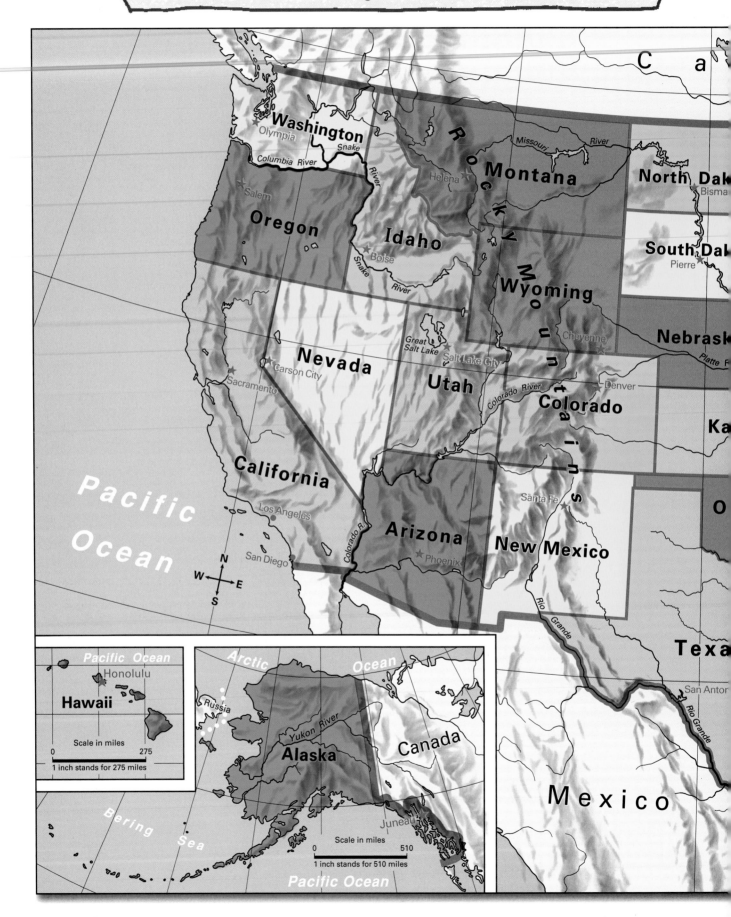

Name the places near your state.

a   d   a

Lake Superior

Minnesota

Wisconsin

St. Paul

Mississippi River

M i c h i g a n

Lake Michigan

Lake Huron

Ottawa

Lake Ontario

Montpelier
Vermont

M o u n t a i n s **Maine**

Augusta

Concord
New Hampshire

Boston

New York

Albany

Lansing

Detroit

Lake Erie

Hartford
Connecticut

Massachusetts

Providence
Rhode Island

Pennsylvania

Iowa

Madison

Des Moines

Chicago

Missouri River

oln

Illinois   **Indiana**

Springfield

Indianapolis

Ohio

Columbus

Harrisburg

Washington, D.C.

New York City

Trenton

New Jersey

Philadelphia

Dover   **Delaware**

Annapolis

peka

Missouri

River

Jefferson City

Ohio River

West

Frankfort   Charleston

Virginia

Maryland

A p p a l a c h i a n   M

Missouri

as

Kentucky

Ohio   River

Virginia

Richmond

Raleigh

Atlantic

homa

Arkansas   River

Arkansas

Nashville

Tennessee

North Carolina

Ocean

homa City

Little Rock

River

Mississippi River

Columbia

South
Carolina

Mississippi

Alabama

Atlanta

Georgia

Dallas

Louisiana

Jackson

Montgomery

N

Baton Rouge

Tallahassee

W   E

ustin

Houston

F l o r i d a

S

Gulf   of   Mexico

Cuba

What was the United

A **1500s and earlier** American Indian pueblo at Taos, New Mexico

Do people still live here?

How can you tell?

B **1600s** British colony at Jamestown, Virginia

States like long ago?

C **1700s** Spanish mission near the California coast

D **1800s** American frontier town at New Salem, Illinois

What was YOUR community like long ago?

What symbols stand for

Washington, D.C., is the capital of the United States of America.

The White House, home of the President

Washington Monument

The flag of the United States

Which of these symbols is in YOUR community?

Washington, D.C.

Why are so many national symbols in Washington, D.C.?

U.S. Capitol, the building where Congress meets

Lincoln Memorial

Who are Americans

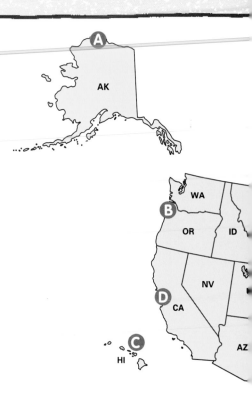

A Alaska

B Oregon

> Is there any place where Americans do NOT come from?

C Hawaii

D California

E Wyoming

today?

F Minnesota

G Illinois

H Pennsylvania

Describe YOUR family and friends.

I Texas

J Georgia

What do people do in

North America

▪▪▪▪▪	Continental boundary
⸺	International boundary
South America	Continent
Bahamas	Country
● Dallas	City
✳ Mexico City	National capital

Scale in miles
0 ⸻ 770

1 inch stands for 770 miles

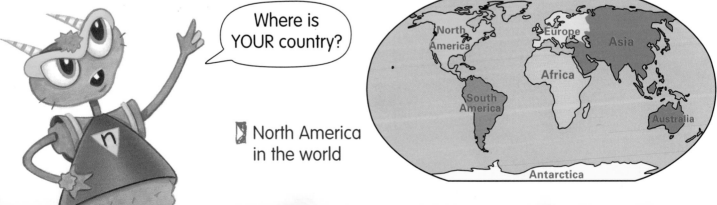

Where is YOUR country?

North America in the world

Buying bananas in Guatemala

Making shoes in Mexico

Use the map to find the places in the photos.

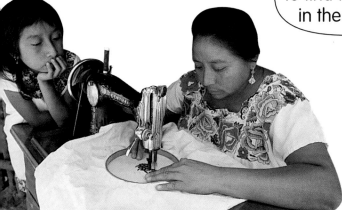
Embroidering cloth in Mexico

Biking in Canada

Herding cattle in Cuba

What do people do in

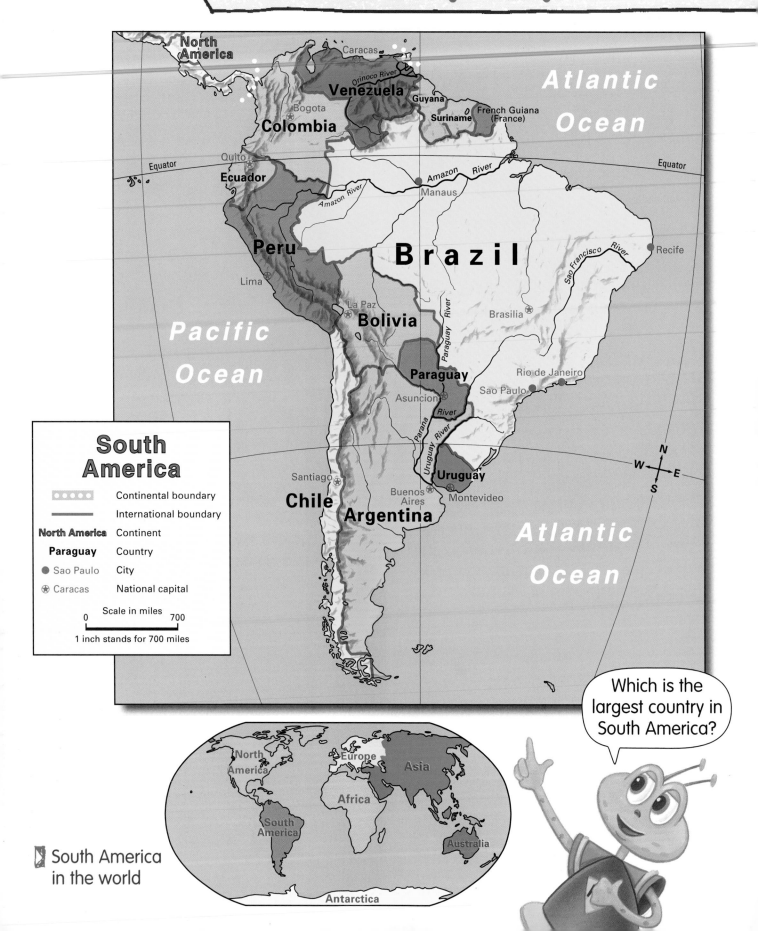

South America

∘∘∘∘∘	Continental boundary
——	International boundary
North America	Continent
Paraguay	Country
● Sao Paulo	City
⊛ Caracas	National capital

Scale in miles
0   700
1 inch stands for 700 miles

Which is the largest country in South America?

South America in the world

Playing wooden flutes in Bolivia

Picking coffee beans in Colombia

Minding a store in Brazil

What does this man sell?

Making plywood in Peru

Walking in a park in Argentina

What do people do in

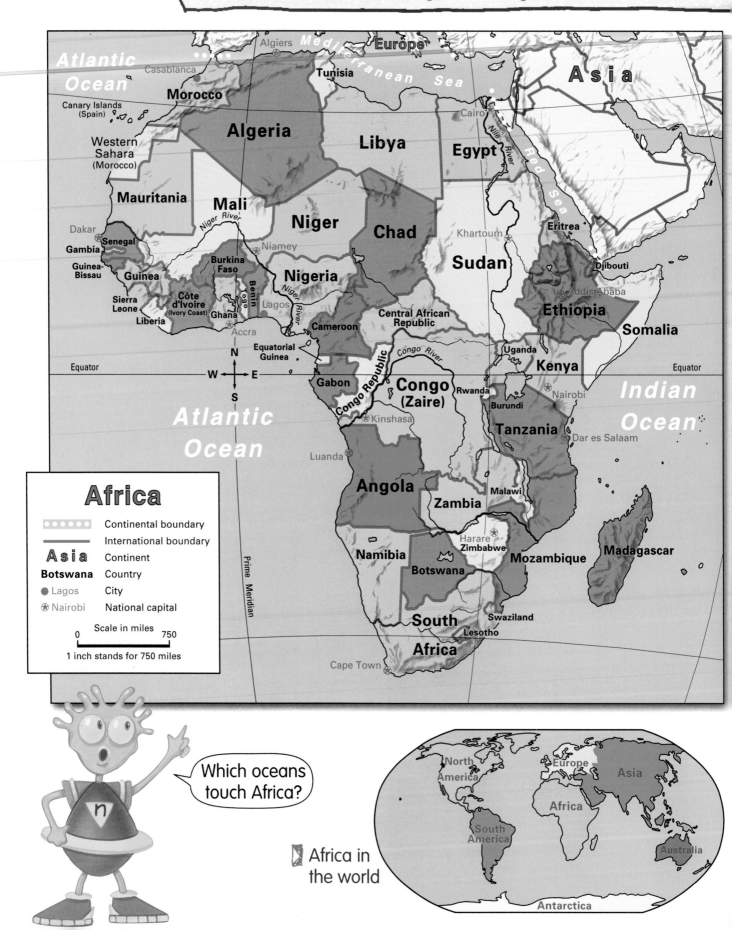

Africa in the world

Which oceans touch Africa?

Playing dominoes in Egypt

Bundling millet in Senegal

How is this store like the one where YOUR family shops?

Picking tea in Kenya

Shopping in South Africa

Polishing diamonds in Botswana

What do people do in

Buying vegetables in Russia

Assembling a motorcycle
in Germany

Can a country
be in two
continents?

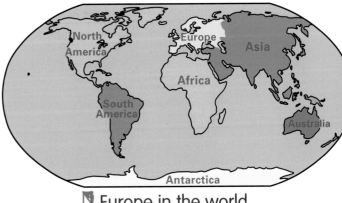

Europe in the world

What is YOUR favorite book?

Europe

○○○○○	Continental boundary
———	International boundary
Asia	Continent
Ukraine	Country
● Istanbul	City
✪ Berlin	National capital

Scale in miles

0   425

1 inch stands for 425 miles

▷ Reading a story in Albania

▷ Playing bagpipes in the United Kingdom

▷ Picking grapes in France

Selling vegetables in India

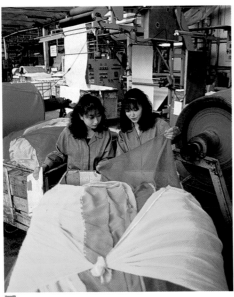

Making cloth in Japan

Are any continents larger than Asia?

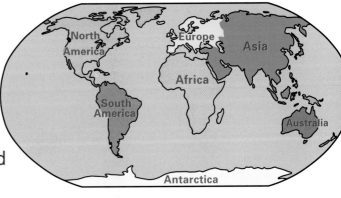

Asia in the world

Asia?

Asia

○○○○○○○	Continental boundary
——	International boundary
Africa	Continent
Thailand	Country
● Karachi	City
⊛ Baghdad	National capital

Scale in miles

0   950

1 inch stands for 950 miles

▷ Playing chess in Uzbekistan

▷ Studying at home in Saudi Arabia

Where do you do YOUR homework?

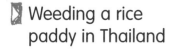

▷ Weeding a rice paddy in Thailand

What do people do in

Herding sheep near Adelaide

Painting in Alice Springs

Is Australia a country, a continent, or both?

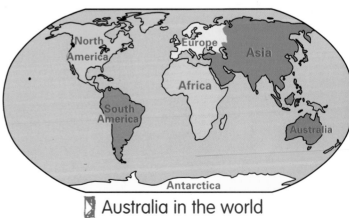

Australia in the world

Australia?

> We get lessons from Nystro the same way!

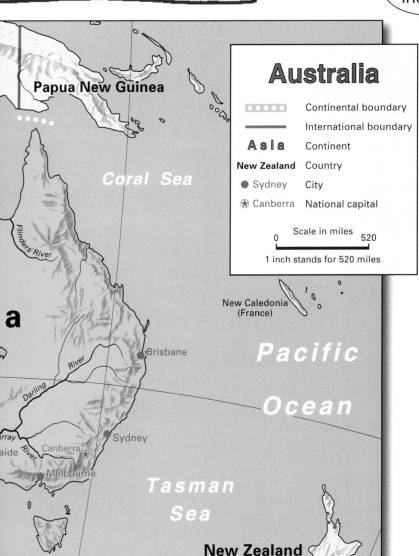

Australia

○○○○○	Continental boundary
——	International boundary
Asia	Continent
New Zealand	Country
● Sydney	City
✪ Canberra	National capital

Scale in miles

0   520

1 inch stands for 520 miles

Papua New Guinea

Coral Sea

Flinders River

a

New Caledonia
(France)

River

Darling

Brisbane

Pacific

Ocean

Murray River

Canberra

Sydney

laide

Melbourne

Tasman
Sea

New Zealand

Teaching school over the radio

Making felt for hats near Sydney

Flying kites near Melbourne

What do people do in

Visiting the coast

Do any people really make their homes in Antarctica?

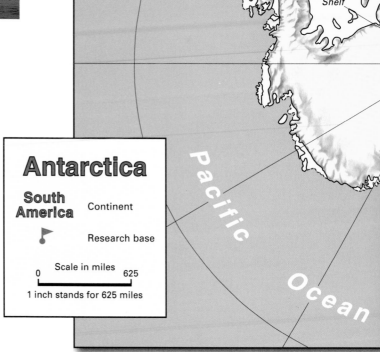

South America

Atlanti

Ice Shelf

Pacific

Ocean

Antarctica

South America Continent

Research base

Scale in miles
0 ————————— 625

1 inch stands for 625 miles

Rafting near icebergs

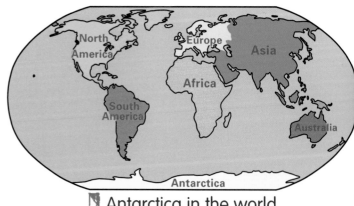

North America

Europe

Asia

Africa

South America

Australia

Antarctica

Antarctica in the world